"SYCHAR, AN HOLINESS CAMP MEETING."

by

W.W. CARY

First Fruits Press
Wilmore, Kentucky
c2015

Sychar: An Holiness Camp Meeting, by W.W. Cary

First Fruits Press, ©2015
Previously published by the Pentecostal Publishing Company, 1933.

ISBN: 9781621712541 (print), 9781621712558 (digital), 9781621712565 (kindle)

Digital version at http://place.asburyseminary.edu/firstfruitsheritagematerial/106/

For all other uses, contact:

First Fruits Press
B.L. Fisher Library
Asbury Theological Seminary
204 N. Lexington Ave.
Wilmore, KY 40390
http://place.asburyseminary.edu/firstfruits

Cover design by John Ramsey

asburyseminary.edu
800.2ASBURY
204 North Lexington Avenue
Wilmore, Kentucky 40390

First Fruits
THE ACADEMIC OPEN PRESS OF ASBURY SEMINARY

First Fruits Press
The Academic Open Press of Asbury Theological Seminary
204 N. Lexington Ave., Wilmore, KY 40390
859-858-2236
first.fruits@asburyseminary.edu
asbury.to/firstfruits

"SYCHAR,

An Holiness Camp Meeting."

W. W. CARY.

PENTECOSTAL PUBLISHING COMPANY, LOUISVILLE, KENTUCKY.

DEDICATION

To one whose life has been more eloquent proof of the great central doctrine of entire sanctification than the greatest Sychar sermon; who in children's and young people's work has served Camp Sychar for a third of a century; who has been the acknowledged exemplar of holy living in all the beauty of holiness throughout Central Ohio; to whose wise guidance and friendship I owe eternal gratitude; to May C. Gorsuch, I respectfully dedicate this book.

Wilmore, Kentucky.

July 10, 1933.

MAY GORSUCH

INTRODUCTION

The typical magazine or newspaper writer of today, who always puts that wonderful word conversion into the quotation marks of scorn, displays similar abysmal ignorance of American history by belittling Camp Meetings, and usually makes the assumption that such meetings are a curious phenomenon of the past, long since outgrown by modern wisdom.

Many stories of the religious movements of America published within the past two decades speak of camp meetings as though they had flourished in pioneer days and were entirely extinct with the coming of the modern era. To readers of such false statements it will be interesting to know that in this decade of the nineteen thirties Americans are privileged to attend more than eight hundred camp meetings wholly evangelistic in purpose. There is scarcely a state in the Union without one or more such meetings each summer. Starting in the East with Freeport, Long Island, and going to the fartherest coast of the Pacific Ocean, the ten days or two weeks wholly devoted to prayer meetings, testimony meetings, children's services, ring meetings and at least three full evangelistic services with sermons and altar services daily, bear witness to the fact that God has His testimony among us to this day. Please God, such testimony shall continue until Christ Himself return to gather to Himself His people.

"Understanding is a wellspring of life unto him that hath it: but the instruction of fools is folly." Prov. 16:22. Every year thousands of hungry-hearted heed the cry "To your tents, O Israel" and hear the gospel preached in God's beautiful outdoors.   .

In the autobiography of Peter Cartwright he says, "There were no camp meetings in regular form at this time. . . . From 1801 for years a blessed revival of religion spread through almost the entire inhabited parts of western

Kentucky, Tennessee, the Carolinas and many other parts.
. . . In this revival originated our camp meeting and in
both the denominations (Presbyterian and Methodist) they
were held every year. . . . ." He refers to Cane Ridge Revival.

In the Life of A. L. P. Green, an early Methodist itiner-
ant, camp meetings are reported to take place in spring,
summer and fall. Often he attended a quarterly meeting
which turned into a camp meeting as the Spirit of God came
down. Camp meetings were much used of God to build the
evangelistic churches. An early camp meeting in Indiana in
the summer of 1829 is hostilely described by Mrs. Trollope
as follows:

"Four high frames, constructed in the form of altars,
were placed at the four corners of the enclosure; on these
were supported layers of earth and sod, on which burned
immense fires of blazing pinewood. On one side a rude platform was erected to accommodate the preachers, fifteen of
whom attended a meeting, and with very short intervals for
necessary refreshment and private devotion, preached in
rotation, day and night from Tuesday to Saturday."

There were no tabernacles. Preaching took place from
stands at the earliest camps. With little preliminary notice
a camp meeting would start wherever there was a cleared
space in the forest.

Perhaps nothing is more genuinely true to the folk-ways
of America than the camp meeting. Their histories are
most valuable, not only to record religious, but also national
progress of our people.

Undoubtedly one of the greatest camp meetings in
America today is that of Camp Sychar at Mt. Vernon, Ohio,
which for two-thirds of a century has held annual meetings.
From its foundation to date it has stood uncorrupted as an
interdenominational HOLINESS camp, hewing straight to
the line with sanctified common sense and singleness of
purpose.

Its converts cover the globe as missionaries, preachers

and lay folk. Wherever you see a Sycharite you will note spiritual fervor and godly life. It is not too imaginative to assert that in the Kingdom of our dear Lord Camp Sychar folk will re-assemble some day as a special group.

This story seeks to honor Camp Sychar and the mighty Holiness Movement in America, owned of God; indeed begun and carried on under the guidance and inspiration of the Holy Spirit.

Recently one denomination sought to emphasize the office of the Holy Spirit and proclaimed the need to get back to Pentecost. Such a need is manifest. But the great Holiness camp meetings spread all over America were never pointed out as the places best fitted to aid the hungry hearted. So this emphasis came to nought.

It is the writer's hope that some good Christians who know they need a deeper work of grace will read this book, and thereby be guided to some Holiness camp meeting where the Gospel of full salvation is still preached according to the Word of God.

One of America's great cartoonists, "Billy" Ireland, of the Columbus Dispatch, recently issued a wonderful picture of a man lost in the mountains of crime, greed, immorality, and moral and economic depression. He cries out, "We lack leadership! What we need is a good leader!" But behind him Human History says, "You've had a LEADER for two thousand years. The trouble is you've turned your back on Him," and points to the shining figure of Jesus Christ.

So, reader, turn back to Christ the Saviour. Read the Word and note the emphasis on "Be ye holy as I am holy." Then turn from work and play, from all the regular routine of life; pack up the family and betake yourselves to Camp Sychar, Eaton Rapids, Richland, Indian Springs, or the nearest camp that is now preaching "Holiness unto the Lord."

CONTENTS

CHAPTER I.

THE BEGINNING

Camp Sychar is the result of a great re-awakening on Scriptural Holiness that swept over America from a meeting held at Vineland, N. J., in 1867; which inaugurated the National Camp Meeting Movement for the promotion of Christian Holiness; a movement that covered the nation.

William MacDonald in his "Life of John S. Inskip," says, "For several years prior to 1867, it was evident to all careful observers that there was not only this sad declension in spirituality in the churches, but that there was a growing opposition to the subject of entire sanctification as a distinct experience. This opposition came from both pulpit and pew and was often met with at the local camp meetings. Rev. John A. Wood, an earnest advocate of "perfect love," expressed his feelings on the subject to Mrs. Harriet E. Drake insisting that a camp for the special promotion of holiness ought to be held.

In discussion with W. B. Osborn and later with John S. Inskip a camp meeting was appointed for Vineland, N. J., July 17-26, 1867. At this camp the National Camp Meeting Association was born. At this meeting Rev. B. W. Gorham, of Newark, N. J., preached. The Holy Spirit was present in great blessing.

The same B. W. Gorham, still under the inspiration of historic Vineland camp, visited Canton, Ohio, in November, 1867 for a few days rest. He preached one Sunday evening and the pastor, without consulting him or anyone, announced he would preach every night of the coming week. To quote from the original minutes, "The meeting so unceremoniously begun, continued some three weeks; resulting in the conversion of a number of souls, and the entire sanctification of several of the members of the church. Rev. Ephraim Ball, or Col. Ball, was one of the latter class.

He had been a local preacher for twenty-five years. But

God wrought a wonderful change in his character, his views and the whole current of his life when He gave him full salvation. His preaching henceforth was all aglow with the fire of perfect love; and contributed much to spread the holy flame among the people of Stark County and neighboring places.

Rev. Gorham went from Canton to Mt. Union where at Mt. Union College twenty were entirely sanctified, including one professor and twelve young men studying for the ministry. The fire spread. Other holiness services were arranged near Canton and Col. Ball established a weekly meeting in that city for the promotion of holiness; and he was impressed that the newly sanctified and earnest seekers must have a few days set aside "to compare views, pray with and for each other and listen to detailed instruction on the doctrine, experience and practice of holiness." A meeting, called a home camp meeting, was arranged for April, 1870, at Alliance, Ohio, to continue five days. Many were converted and over one hundred persons professed perfect love.

On the last day of the meeting a State camp meeting for the promotion of holiness was proposed and much discussed. A committee, with Col. E. Ball chairman and including G. W. Dennis, Hiram Miller and of course, B. W. Gorham, met and arranged the first full camp meeting at the Fair Grounds, Canton, which began August 23, 1870, and lasted ten days. The first pamphlet announcing the meeting stated as the object: "The special object of this meeting is the promotion of the doctrine and experience of Christian Holiness." Col. E. Ball had offered to take the whole financial responsibility of this meeting and he purchased a tabernacle at a cost of $450.00.

Here the Ohio State Camp Meeting Association was formally organized. B. W. Gorham, Sheridan Baker, Hiram Miller and G. W. Dennis preached—all familiar names to the attendants of the next decade.

There was a Joseph Smith of the Philadelphia Conference who preached; but Joseph H. Smith told the writer it could not be he, since that date was three years before he was converted.

An effort to raise funds gave an excellent result: More than $520.00 was pledged and (words so acceptable to camp meeting treasurers) "most of them paid in cash." The meeting ended with the sacrament of the Lord's Supper and a march around the grounds, also called a "march around Jerusalem." Board and preachers led a procession, two and two of all the people, once or more in a complete circuit of the camp grounds and then the leader stood still while the next man passed him, shook hands, and then stood beside him. Each in turn did the same so that every person shook hands with every other one. This was a custom in the National Camps and still is done in some holiness camp meetings, notably at Eaton Rapids, Michigan. It would be interesting to see it revived at Camp Sychar.

The camp meetings continued at Canton Fair Grounds. In all early meetings there were many preachers. The second camp had twenty-six different preachers. A resolution at the November Association meeting reads: "that the executive committee do not employ ministerial aid which involves expense, except under extraordinary circumstances." Dr. and Mrs. Phoebe Palmer preached at this meeting. They were counted "extraordinary circumstances" to the amount of $30.00 and board.

At the second meeting children's separate services were inaugurated. There was no tabernacle as later erected. Like the older camp meetings there was a preacher's stand in front of which was room for seekers in an inclosed space. Each service had two speakers—the preacher and the exhorter. There must have been times of great victory, for this significant resolution occurs: "Resolved that any member of the Association shall be at liberty to order delay of a few minutes in the ringing of the bell at the Stand at the close of a service, when in his judgment the interests of the meeting then being held, demand it."

There was one service held in German and a special service for preachers' wives.

From the very beginning, as indicated above, the plainly stated object was entire sanctification of believers. In the announcement of the first camp was this "Invitation": "Come. Our object is salvation, present full salvation, God's fire in human hearts, the consuming, purging fire. This we feel must save the Church and save the world. Thousands in all churches are groping and guessing and stumbling in the twilight, and nothing but the baptism of fire can save them. Reader, are you one of these? If so, come to the Ohio State Camp Meeting and look for your Pentecost. If not, if God has given you full salvation, then get a little lower at the feet of Jesus than you ever were before, and come in His name and strength to help your brethren. Come and bring the household. Come at the beginning. Come to stay. Come to wait and work in God's orders."

This would make a very good invitation to this day. The statement of twilight conditions appertains. The emphasis, "Come and bring the Household. Come at the beginning. Come to stay," is also greatly needed. Very little of the grace of God comes to those who visit a camp meeting on the wing, and behave as though awaiting a train. To drive in late; enter the service after the glorious singing and praying is over; to race off hurriedly the moment the altar call is given; how often does this conduct negative the convicting power of faithful preaching. "The Lord is good unto them that wait for Him, to the soul that seeketh Him." Lam. 3:25. God will be enquired of by man. None would dash in and out of the presence of an earthly king so rudely. How often has the Holy Spirit of God refrained from His blessed work of conviction upon the soul of an unawakened Laodicean, headed for perdition, because, "We must leave right now, Martha. Remember, we have to drive twenty-five miles yet tonight. I can't help it if the preacher has asked that none leave. Come on, hurry."

Very early in its history the Association made a complete, plain, unmistakable statement of its foundation belief and purpose as follows:

"OUR PLATFORM AND OUR WORK"

"Brethren beloved, partakers of like precious faith! We believe you and ourselves solemnly called by the providence and grace of God to great and special efforts for the spread of Scriptural Holiness in these lands. Our platform as to doctrine embraces exactly the points held and specially emphasized by John Wesley during the last thirty years of his life, and held and maintained also by the acknowledged standard writers of Methodism, such as Watson, Adam Clarke, Benson, Fletcher, Asbury, Hamline, Peck and others.

"The same points are maintained substantially by the men of other churches who have written from heart experience of full salvation. Mahan, Finney, Upham, Boardman are examples.

"They and we believe and therefore teach that:—

"1.   The scriptural expressions 'Perfect love,' 'entire sanctification,' 'purity of heart,' 'perfection,' 'complete in Him,' are substantially equivalent expressions, as implying the complete purification of the heart of a believer from unholy tempers and affections by the power of the Holy Spirit.

"2.   That this complete purification of the heart is a distinct experience from conversion and is subsequent thereto in point of time.

"3.   That it is received instantaneously in the same sense as the new birth, or a natural birth or the making of a covenant, or the process of dying is instantaneous.

"4.   That like justification, regeneration and adoption it is received and held by faith.

"5.   That the profession of the blessing is to be made, where it is enjoyed in all humility and yet with frequency and Christian boldness.

"We propose this year as we have in the years before to hold a meeting for the inculcation of these views, but more especially for the purpose of leading believers into the precious experience of heart purity. We expect also, as before, to witness many conversions."

What occasion have the present and future generations to praise God the Father for these faithful men who hewed to the line with that firm undeviating testimony to the mighty truth, that a believer in Christ can indeed be cleansed from all sin and receive a perfect heart of love toward God. They have borne witness to us that Christ's promise, "And I will pray the Father that he shall give you another Comforter, that he may abide with you forever; even the Spirit of truth . . ." is fulfilled. Blessed be our Christ forever. He abides even now in His fulness.

CHAPTER II.

THE YEARS OF PILGRIMAGE

In January, 1873, Col. Ball went home as the earliest of that mighty Sychar band, which without doubt, will foregather sometime in Heaven for a special praise service before the throne of the Lamb of God. He is to be counted as one of the Founders. What a reward will he share when all the hosts of those saved and sanctified in these camps gather among the redeemed.

It may have been because of his death that Canton was abandoned as a site. There had been money difficulties. A resolution authorized a small loan at not to exceed 12% interest. Sheridan Baker loaned the Association $500.00 to clear liabilities. Some of the equipment was sold. The tents were rented to Lakeside Camp Meeting Association.

Apparently in 1873 things were difficult and the enthusiasm for the new enterprise fell to a low ebb. Finances were precarious. Col. Ball's excellent connections were largely lost by his decease. Attendance at the annual meeting fell off badly. A committee was appointed to consider Mansfield Fair Grounds for the 1874 camp. Their report reads rather forlornly. There were old buildings to be removed. Everything was much neglected. The ground was overgrown with weeds and bushes. The water supply was unsatisfactory.

Let us get the complete picture. A victorious union and a rapidly expanding west had carried a colossal boom through America for almost a decade. Great extravagances brought the usual aftermath. The great panic of 1873 began in July and held the country in a paralyzing grip for four years and longer. Men of large vision looked with despair on the future. Great enterprises backed with millions totally ceased to exist. Yet in the very earliest days of this panic, when all men's hearts were failing them for fear, a group of poor men, mostly preachers, dared go on

with God by faith, in the face of every discouragement in
the camp meeting enterprise.

God was able to stimulate some one or more with courage
to go on. The record is very brief. There are hints that
Sheridan Baker, feeble in health but filled with the Holy
Ghost, was that one. The fifth camp meeting took place at
Mansfield Fair Grounds. This note occurs, "S. Baker
preached to the 'Newly Sanctified' with powerful effect. It
became very apparent that the Holy Spirit put His seal upon
the discourse. Quite a number during this camp were sanctified and a number justified." The record indicates that
the time before this camp was the low ebb in the fortunes
of the Association.

At the annual meeting that fall David Updegraff, Friend,
was added to the board. A resolution leading to a new de-
parture authorized two camps for 1875. The Board must
have been much encouraged to double its total meetings.
While there have been difficult situations since, there never
have been any signs of the defeatist spirit since the 1873
annual meeting. All Sycharites have reason to be thankful
to the Joshua, strong and of a good courage, who in the face
of every discouragement said, "Brethren, let us go on. God
has blessed us. Conversions and sanctifications are the
proof of His approval. We must not fail the hungry hearted
who need our ministry. If God be for us, who can be
against us."

The sixth camp meeting, at Mansfield began to reward
such faith and courage. The president, Rev. Hiram Miller,
and Sheridan Baker, vice president, were both at home sick.
Dr. A. Lowry, of Philadelphia, Bishop Andrews, and A. B.
Leonard of Cincinnati, preached. One service held in the
open lasted eight hours without interruption. "Much good
was done. Several preachers preached."

Further notes of victory: "Bro. Leonard preached with
powerful effect, having received the Baptism of full salvation at the last Urbana camp. It has been estimated that
nearly one hundred persons have received the blessing of

Holiness at this meeting and a goodly number have been justified."

This again displays the close link between the Ohio Association and the great National Holiness Camp Meeting movement, which was sweeping the country these years. Urbana was the site of four of the first fifty National camps, thereby being the most frequently used camp in America. Here Inskip and MacDonald wrought powerfully in the Lord. No wonder Leonard was moved to seek and find.

Incidentally an invitation was extended to the National group to take charge of the Ohio Association 1876 meeting, with Inskip, MacDonald, Boole and Lowry specially invited.

The rising tide is manifest: "A communication of fraternal greetings and precious Christian experiences while under severe bodily affliction was received from Dr. S. Baker and read on Sunday morning in the Love Feast producing a marvelous effect."

"The relation at the Love Feast of the miraculous cure of a sister in Mansfield was hailed as the result of a perfect trust in the Messiah of Bethany and the fact was verified by a number of witnesses."

"On Tuesday after the close of meeting, Sister Medill held a prayer meeting of three hours in the altar, resulting in much good."

There had been trouble as well. A gang of rowdies molested the meeting, resulting in legal prosecution of two ring leaders, who resisted arrest. This is an echo of an old American pioneer custom. The records of almost every early camp meeting attendant, that have come down to us, tell of bands of drunken rioters, who try to break up the meeting. Peter Cartwright's "Autobiography" relates many curious expedients he employed to defeat their purposes. The "good old days" were also exceedingly bad old days in the Ohio and Mississippi valleys.

But the camp ended with a Lord's Supper at which thirty-eight ministers and 435 people partook. The entire congregation took an unanimous vote requesting the return of the Association to Mansfield. What a contrast to that forlorn and disheartened committee looking over a semi-abandoned, weed covered grove and wondering whether it was worth while to go on.

To those in Holiness work facing the appalling financial outlook of the "Great Depression" at this writing; and to those who will surely repeat such experiences in the coming generations, if our Lord tarries; this condition and its glorious resultant triumph is offered as a proof that the saints of God "out of weakness were made strong, waxed valiant in fight, turned to flight the armies of aliens." It is a powerful tendency of human thought to add heroic and unusual qualities to the great saints of the past. "But God hath chosen the foolish things of the world to confound the things which are mighty."

If the feeble Ohio Association, new and with very little prestige, could face the terrible postwar panic of 1873 and its paralysis, which lasted so long and was so violent, and win through under the banner of Holiness; surely the camps, schools and colleges, evangelists and editors of the great Holiness Movement of today and the future can survive any outside influences of disaster, and continue to bear witness that the blood of Jesus Christ, His Son, cleanseth from all sin. Glory to His name.

The year 1876 inaugurated multiple meetings. The first was held at Mansfield in August and a second meeting followed in September at Hollow Rock. This year Amanda Smith, a name later much associated with these camps, was invited to preach, but could not come. At the annual meeting, three Ohio towns applied for camps; Oberlin, Warren and Canton. It was agreed that there would be three camps the next year. Multiple camps seemed a success.

It was at this annual meeting that Rev. J. W. Hill, for so many years a standby of the Association, was elected a member. It began an activity that continued unbroken to his death.

Hollow Rock was in some legal difficulties relative to

possession of the grounds, so the meeting could not be repeated there, although cordially urged to return.

The 1877 campaigns brought some nationally known figures to Ohio. Dr. Daniel Steele, J. W. Luccock, and J. A. Wood, co-founder of the National camp meeting work and author of "Perfect Love," were present and preached. At one meeting or another the O. S. C. M. A. have employed every national evangelist of note in the Holiness Movement. The register of preachers at its camps is a roster of the Movement in America.

J. W. HILL

In the earliest camps members of the Association did most of the preaching. Toward the end of the seventies it is noticeable that outside talent is increasingly in evidence.

In 1879 in the face of invitations to many communities, camps were held at Youngstown and Delaware. A motion was carried to lease land at Delaware for five years. This might have resulted in permanent location in that important Methodist educational center, but certain factors arose to cancel the move. Only one Ohio Wesleyan professor is noted as a preacher in a day when the faculty of the college were

notably evangelistic. This was Professor McCabe. A significant motion after the Delaware camp hints at opposition
encountered. It was moved at the annual meeting of 1879
that the President confer with pastors and presiding elder
at Delaware and try to secure co-operation in the camp
meeting to be held there.

Apparently the effort failed. Perhaps ecclesiasticism
reared one of its multiple heads. At all events there was
only one more meeting there and the five year lease plan
failed. Thus this great holiness camp meeting began in
very vital alliance with the Methodist College at Mt. Union
and later was closely associated with O. W. U. What
changed histories these colleges might have shown had this
relationship been maintained. It would be interesting to
observe the reaction the faculty of these schools would dis-
play today, if a proposal came before them to assist the es-
tablishment of an holiness camp meeting in their neighbor-
hoods.

It was at the 1879 annual meeting that A. S. Caton became interested in the camps. His godly activity contributed much to the meetings so long as he was in Ohio. He
was notable for sound judgment and wise counsel in financial and operating matters.

After three successful camps in 1880 at Delaware, Cosh-
octon and Youngstown, the improving financial status is
shown as the assets are set forth at $2,556.00. Hiram
Miller was succeeded as president by Sheridan Baker.
Cleveland, Columbus and a number of other cities asked for
a camp. Dr. Lowry proposed that the Association find and
establish a permanent location and a Committee began its
search which was to last six years before a decision came.
In 1882 it was moved that the committee consider the
"grounds of Judson Ball, living between Fredericktown and
Mt. Vernon, with a view to securing said grounds by lease
or otherwise, wherein to locate our camp meeting." This is
the first mention of Mt. Vernon as a possible site.

In 1883 after a camp meeting at Orrville the Association

went outside the borders of Ohio and held a camp at Frank-
lin, Pa. This is strongly in contrast with everything the
Association has ever done before or since. So widely at
variance is this with the later policy, when even a member
of the Association automatically was dropped when he
moved his residence outside of Ohio, save under very unusual circumstances.

The camp meetings continued at Orrville down to and
including a first camp in 1887. In the eighties the Olivers
are noted as very active workers and Prof. R. E. Hudson
is listed annually as in charge of the song service. It is
typical of the O. S. C. M. A. to hold certain persons responsi-
ble for song leadership, young people's meetings and children's services for a period of years. Evangelists change
much more frequently.

At Orrville in 1886 a memorial service was held for
Maggie Baker, who for so many years had labored faithfully with the children. Her name will ever be on the roll
of remembrance among Sychar's children with that of Mrs.
Oliver and Miss Mae Gorsuch.

CHAPTER III.

ON SYCHAR GROUNDS

In 1885 it was noted that G. W. Ball was now Presiding Elder at Mt. Vernon. Perhaps because of that fact the annual meeting was held there in November, 1886, and at that meeting two notable names in the Association's history appear as Rev. J. S. Reager, pastor of the Gay Street M. E. Church of Mt. Vernon, and R. A. Schmuck were elected members. Bro. Reager, a very forceful man and boldly a preacher of full salvation, was forthwith made a member of the Executive Committee. T. H. Seymour, of Mt. Vernon, and A. S. Caton were elected as lay members. Thus there were three residents of Mt. Vernon on the Board.

The addition of so much splendid leadership and driving force made itself manifest rapidly. At this annual meeting a queer and uncomfortable condition was noted. The physical assets of the Association were shown to be scattered widely in different towns and places. Some things were in a stable, some in a tent house on a farm; others in Fair Grounds buildings in still another location. A discussion of this situation confirmed the Board's resolution to abandon its peripatetic character and establish a permanent location.

After a camp meeting at Orrville the last of July, 1887, in which Rev. Reager preached often and displayed much zeal for the work, on August 24 the Association had its first great camp meeting on the sacred grounds of Camp Sychar.

Right here the reader must bear with me for a moment. How I do praise God for His wonderful goodness and mercy to me and to all within a day's journey of Mt. Vernon. Then indeed a light of the gospel of full salvation burst upon all the people round about. "In Him was life; and the life was the light of men. And the light shineth in darkness."

How sadly true is the often repeated statement of good

church people, "I never heard of the privilege of sanctification for believers. For long years since my conversion, I
have been hungry hearted, feeling a lack, but knowing not

SCENE AT CAMP SYCHAR

the way." Or "the only preaching I ever heard on the subject was an exaggerated fanatical, non-Biblical distortion
of this mighty truth, that would alienate any honest follower

of Jesus Christ." But no man nor woman of Knox County,
Ohio, can ever say they lacked an opportunity to hear full
salvation expounded clearly, faithfully and year after year
as men of God, obviously filled with the Holy Spirit preached
the Word; witnessed to the work done; explained difficulties away; prayed fervently, and held an open altar of
blessing for every seeker.

O sacred altar of Sychar. Happy are the people who
have knelt humbly in the straw and mourned, hungering
and thirsting after righteousness until they were filled.

The cross of Christ and the opened sepulchre stand at the
head of all sacred objects. But to the upper room at Jerusalem, the Wittenberg church door of Luther and the Fet-
ter Lane church of Wesley must be added the altar of
Sychar; for there God has come down with mighty power
and blessing upon men.

The straw of Bethlehem's manger and the straw of
Sychar's altar will both be sung in the new hymnology of
eternity, when the saints gather to praise the Lamb that
was slain.

That hot August day of 1887, a quiet farmer's wife drove
into Mt. Vernon alone, against the opposition of her husband, and stopped to tell her daughter-in-law that there was
a holiness camp meeting starting in a nearby grove and she
wanted her to get in the buggy and go. "But what shall I
do with my baby? He is only four months old." "Wrap
him up and bring him along," said this mother in Israel,
who would not be denied. So my mother obeyed and carried
me to my first holiness camp meeting the first year on
Sychar's grounds. To the far limits of eternity I will still
be praising God for Camp Sychar. So will many another
boy and girl, likewise given the privilege of hearing the
gospel with the unction of the Holy Spirit, an unction the
eager ear of childhood so readily recognizes.

That grandmother is now in the presence of our Lord
with joy forever and her earthly tenement rests near Bangs
on the Columbus Road. I never pass that grave without

uttering the pledge, "I am going through, under the white banner of Holiness, by the grace of God."

She told me her husband, later saved by her faithful prayers, objected strongly. It was all foolishness to go off ten days to a camp meeting in the busiest part of a farmer's year. Harvest season usually came about Sychar time, and anyone familiar with a farm knows what the coming of the thrashers means. They would be ruined. She said, "I resolved I would go at any money cost. In all the years God has prospered us and we never have even lost money, though I was willing to do so. Take time to seek after God. Go to camp meeting, no matter what interferes. Attend the preaching and the prayer meetings. Sit up in front. Take part. Get into the spirit of the camp and God will bless you." That is sound doctrine and exhortation.

This first camp meeting on Sychar grounds was the twenty-seventh camp held and the seventeenth year of the Association. Multiple meetings account for the discrepancy. For the benefit of early attendants some of the program may be brought to remembrance. Mrs. Synder had the children's services and G. F. Oliver was in charge of the young people. The 5:30 A. M. prayer services and the testimony services were largely conducted by board members and visiting preachers. G. W. Ball, A. S. Caton, G. W. Dennis and Impertus Martin are some of these. The latter had from an early date acted as layman manager and secretary in charge of grounds and physical property. A Canton man, he was a strong factor in the promotion of the meetings. Later his duties were divided among several. The venerable Father Kellum, a superannuated circuit rider living in Mt. Vernon, had one service at this camp.

The regular preaching services were in the hands of Baker, Reager and Dennis of the Association and the outside evangelists were McCauley and Dr. E. Crouston. Sheridan Baker preached the most frequently with G. W. Dennis next. There is a note during the meeting that Orrville brethren have now organized their own holiness camp meeting. Their action is heartily approved and Orrville is no longer in Sychar Association's care. Hereafter there is only one camp a year and always at Sychar grounds.

For years there had been talk of incorporation but no action. The evidence is strong that the new members added much vitality to the Board. Incorporation under the laws of the State of Ohio was promptly arranged and a carefully drawn up Constitution and By-laws adopted. The management of the camp was divided so that several Board members had specific responsibility. Grounds, tickets and gates were given in charge of Schmuck, who was long to occupy this post. Oliver was president and Caton secretary, a combination that worked effectively for many years.

With new constitution, new officers, and new grounds, new life began for the Association. The next year's camp, 1888, ends with this significant notation: "Last service, preaching by A. Lowry, followed by grand march and testimony—grandest meeting of our history. Scores saved. *Victory every service.*" The last was heavily underlined. Truly the Holy Ghost appeared and dedicated the Sychar grounds as holy ground where until Our Lord appears, full salvation should be preached, sinners saved, backsliders reclaimed, believers wholly sanctified, and the people of God be freshly anointed with mighty outpourings of the Spirit of God. Please God, so may it be until the Rapture of the saints.

It is to be noted that the custom of "Marching round Jerusalem" at the close of the camp was observed at the first two camps on Sychar.

Perhaps the enemy of our souls saw with dismay what this holy place would mean for the advancement of the Kingdom of Christ, for he began presenting stumbling blocks. Water shortage was very serious. A driven well was begun and at the usual depth it proved a dry hole. I remember clearly the shine on the faces of several early campers as they related the story. No water meant a resumption of their wanderings again; a defeat to all the bright hopes that already had begun to be harbored.

A call to earnest prayer was made. Would to God some one in the darkness of disbelief would read and note this fact. Many a wise philosopher of Anti-Christ has proven to his own, and his deluded followers, satisfaction that all natural phenomena obey certain fixed "laws;" that God, if there be a God, would stultify Himself if He violated His own "law" merely to answer prayer. Hence all prayer is futile, save in creating imaginary mental exaltation, never at all related to cold, hard facts.

Perhaps Sychar folks are too foolish and ignorant to be up on the great philosophic and scientific systems so profoundly worked out. At all events they were simple enough in mind—and faith—to believe that the God who created the earth could command His own works; and that He loved them enough to hear their prayers and answer them. There were even some of these humble, foolish people who still read and believed certain out-dated Jewish writings in a Book and quoted it to prove that where two or three were gathered together in the name of Christ, He Himself was there in invisible presence and blessing. They dared assert that the great creative force, the First Cause, cared for them so individually that each separate hair on their heads had a number known to Him.

How absurd to one who has looked through a great telescope (or read in a book about it) and seen a billion mighty suns swinging majestically in illimitable space. Surely the Creator of all this is too busy to consider the whole race of man, let alone any single individual. But in all history there have been a few, who could not be satisfied with Reason, but always went on to lay hold of the Unknown by faith. They are most stubborn. Perhaps it is best not to argue with them. But why, great thinker, do you ever find your uneasy thoughts brought back to such negligible people? The mighty monarch, Darius, himself lost sleep over one of this lot.

All Sychar met and prayed earnestly to God, that He; who thrust back the waters of the Red Sea and of Jordan;

who commanded the waves of Galilee to cease tossing and walked those waters as on an oaken floor, would once more show His power over one of His created elements and turn water into a dry hole. Some of these saints announced that they had the answer from God before they arose from their knees and calmly asserted that water would flow, even before they saw any.

What a mighty shout presently arose as the messenger rushed up to tell of the gushing of crystal waters in abundant stream from the heretofore dry hole. It flowed forth in that plenitude with which our Father always gives good gifts unto His children—enough and to spare. The well which flowed in the eighteen eighties still pours forth in the nineteen thirties water famous for its crystal purity and peculiarly health-giving qualities.

Perhaps our Lord wished to illustrate to His people that tremendous verse, "He that believeth on me, as the scripture hath said, out of his belly shall flow rivers of living waters. (But this spake He of the Spirit, which they that believe on Him should receive:—)" Is it not the baptism with this same Holy Spirit of God that pours forth so abundantly upon those that come to Sychar grounds earnestly seeking?

CHAPTER IV.

It will be of interest to present a picture of Camp Sychar in the early days. The natural grove of mighty trees, irregularly placed as they grew, had very few saplings and small trees among them. The lines of trees were planted later. The camp was much further from the outmost bounds of Mt. Vernon, for that city's suburbs stopped at Pleasant street, much short of Dry Creek. In the visible surrounding country were only two or three farm houses at a distance. On the grounds the buildings were confined to gate house, book store, grocery stand and the old red tabernacle. There were no dormitories. Children and young people met in a tent. Instead of electric lights there were kerosene flares like those used by street corner pitchmen. They burned fitfully with alternate flare and swish, small blue flame and silence. The "hush, hush, hush" of these flares at spaced intervals mingle with the orchestra of cicadas to bring homesick longings for Sychar, as memories flood back to hundreds scattered over the earth today.

Many a night in Western Canada I have dreamed it all and awakened to entertain sacred remembrances of old Sychar. Is it possible for any of the children, who every year returned thither, ever to get away from profound assurance of the truth of Holiness in any miasmic swamp of unbelief? God grant it may never be.

The children of Sychar! Jim Reager, Howard Oliver, Lewis Akers, Paul Ashbaugh—scores of faces come to mind. It hurts to hear this typical testimony from mature lips: "As a small child in children's meeting I went to the altar and thought I was saved and sanctified. Of course, later, I had to go back and get a real work done in my soul. So at twenty-five after years of wandering I sought and found the blessing."

Such folk are deceived. God did meet them. Their child-ish covenants are recorded in the archives of Heaven. The blood of Jesus Christ cleansed them from all sin, as with

YOUNG PEOPLE'S TENT

simple childlike faith they asked and believed.

I bear witness this day that the covenant entered into with Christ at five years of age at Sychar's children's service has never been broken by Him. I am satisfied that many of His gracious providences in keeping me from out-broken, deadly sin; that that continuous faithful whisper of the Holy Spirit, warning and guiding me; date from that first surrender.

True, I knew very little theology. All I was aware of was that as that gracious, beautiful lady away up there on the platform told us we should love Jesus, my heart said, "That is what I want to do." How easy the path; how few the inhibitions, doubts and fears; how quick the reception by our blessed Saviour. I earnestly believe it is His plan that children should be received and made wholly His before ever they begin an apprenticeship to sin.

There was no children's play ground. After children's meeting, the grown folk went to preaching service. My grandmother's rule for any child staying at her tent was fixed attendance at children's and young people's meetings and one preaching service with her. Never could we go into the back seats at preaching and slip out when we grew tired. Up to the front we marched carrying a chair for her, and sat directly under the preacher's eye. When he thundered out denunciations of wrong doing, it seemed he must surely be directing all his bolts straight at us. If there was needed a trip to the altar, the way was open and the journey short.

I believe that here parents have a duty beyond merely taking the children to camp meeting and vaguely hoping they will get some good. There are devil's short cuts to sin and disobedience on a camp ground. Always, even among those quite young, there are rebellious spirits that pull away from the holy influences and incite others to jeer and scoff at all the oracles of God. A gospel hardened young man, who has gone to Holiness camp meeting all his life and still is in rebellion, is about as dangerous a companion as one could find. Hophni and Phinehas were contemptuously familiar with all the temple of God from their earliest childhood. Doubtless Eli believed in a vague "good influence" that would avail, and forgot that as a parent he owed it to his sons to control, teach and pray with them, until they were in the way of life and knew God from personal experience, not through parental tradition alone.

The back seat, inattentive, giggling, quickly departing group of children without parents; who later report, "Yes, I was at preaching service. Sure, Brother Blank preached and his text was—" but forget to say that they departed with the text's own echoes; such seldom get to the altar. Those boys and girls who are required at camp meeting to sit with elders away up front and who must stay, even though the bench grows hard and uncomfortable, do hear and do receive the precious Word. It is from them that the second and third generations of holiness people develop.

When not in meeting the small children traced moles' burrows in the soft ground; built remarkable castles of cockle burrs; or laid out elaborate ground plans with tent stakes. Older ones buzzed green walnuts up the slanting canvas of the big tent and rejoiced in the whirring return; or organized swimming parties in Dry Creek, where the deepest part at the dam was at least three or four feet deep. Then back to the tent with raging appetite where usually a few apples, cookies, or a piece of pie bridged that awful gaping hour before the whole tentful gathered; some on a bench, some on the cot—grandmother and perhaps an honored guest alone occupying the dignity of chairs—the children at the tent's edge on the floor for the glorious fare typical of Sychar days. Camp meeting fare was just as characteristically recognizable as the red "Indian blanket" that always draped the front tent cot where company sat.

The grown folks were waiting as we straggled in from young people's meeting. The man who lit the flares was on his rounds. We smaller ones were tucked into bed, comforted with a tent flap fastened back, so reducing the distance from the assembly. The cicadas filled in all the spaces between the hush-hush of the torches. Then from the tabernacle came a big hearty voice, "You-all wite folks don't

know how to sing that right. Yo don't open yore mouths
wide enough. Now hear Amanda sing!"

> "When Israel out of Egypt came
> A sea before them lay.
> The Lord reached down His Mighty hand
> And rolled the sea away."

"Sing it, now!" The mighty chorus takes it up:

> "Then forward still, 'tis Jehovah's will
> Though the billows roar and spray—"

Then Joseph Smith's voice, "Beloved, I take my text tonight." Hush-hush. Chirp, chirp. Hush, chirp, h-u-s-h!

What boy in English castle, American millionaire man-
sion or luxurious Adirondack's summer residence ever can
have such glorious childhood memories as the patched over-
all, barefoot boy of Camp Sychar.

Sunday at Sychar. At earliest dawning there is the un-
usually painful scrubbing. Unaccustomed feet, which can
now run across cinders without flinching, are rammed and
crammed into shoes, grown amazingly small and narrow.
The stiff wide white collar blouse, which must not be soiled,
and all the Sunday attire is but the preliminary.

At the gate buggies and wagons are pouring in in an
unbroken dusty stream that reaches beyond sight. The field
above the camp displays row on row of rigs, while owners
lead horses off to a feeding place. At the tent basket after
stuffed basket is slipped into every available cranny, as
Uncle John's family, Aunt Rachel and her children, the
neighbor Browns, etc., pass by.

Near noon hour it is almost impossible to get in to the
well for water. Tenters usually get their water supplies
early. A visit to the long trough with weighted cover,
through which the cool water flows, means careful selection
of one's own butter, milk and watermelon, floating in peace-
ful companionship with a score of others. In every part of
the grounds there are picnic parties at dinner. There is no
fast moving car to drive away in for food. Some of these

families were up before dawn and drove the team three or four hours along dusty country roads to get to camp meeting. If Susy and the baby are yellow with dust; if the boys' unaccustomed shoes have lost all semblance of shine; there is a reason. But father and mother get a full year's spiritual feast out of a day at Sychar.

They never miss coming even though they cannot take a tent. Since father and mother were sanctified at Sychar the plain little farm house has taken on a new peace. No voice of scolding arises on hot summer days. Father never goes off to attend the prolonged sessions at the cross roads store, where much tobacco juice spirts forth and the dirty story is snickeringly told. Instead the children become familiar with the sight of father's gnarled hands leafing over the big Bible; and sometimes he droops forward over it with head on table asleep after a hard day's plowing. There are family prayers. When John got a bit wild, father stopped the plow to kneel in a raspberry-filled fence corner and cry and plead with God to save his boy.

The chickens have often heard a soft voice singing,
"Hallelujah! Hallelujah! I'm so glad to tell;
Hallelujah! Hallelujah! with my soul 'tis well,"
as mother scatters the grain. At the white wooden church everyone knows father is no scholar and constitutionally backward in speech. The school teacher and the country store keeper usually head the arguments on knotty theological points; but every ear is respectfully alert when father does speak; and mother's tear-softened voice in prayer makes all the neighbors tender hearted.

An Ohio farm can be the doorway to the poorhouse; to the mad house; to perdition. But a Spirit-filled couple, though but poor tenants, can make one into Bunyan's Beulah Land, "for in this land the Shining Ones commonly walked, because it was upon the borders of Heaven." From such farms have emerged godly men and women, the very salt of the earth, that today keep America from hopeless corruption.

GLIMPSES

CHAPTER V.

At the first camp on Sychar grounds in 1887 the treasurer estimated total assets at between $2000 and $2500.

In 1888 Martin resigned after years of active service and Schmuck was made treasurer. For 1889 camp meeting invitations to preach were sent to Sam Small for two days; to Dr. A. B. Leonard, Dr. Bayliss and S. A. Keen, then removed to Indianapolis. A new name makes its first appearance among prospective evangelists in the following note:

"Bro. Oliver was instructed to secure services of Rev. Smith as evangelist, *if not too expensive.*"

This was Joseph H. Smith, who for so many years would link his name annually with Sychar services. Of all living evangelists of today he is the only survivor who dates so far back on Sychar's rolls. As honorary president of the National Holiness Association his name for more than a half century has been identified with the preaching of holiness from coast to coast.

He has crossed the continent often enough to circle the globe ten times. He is giving his ripest ministry in these latter days.

Sychar has had so many seasons of Joseph Smith's preaching that many old campers think of him whenever they think of camp meeting.

The following year William Chase acted as reporter. He also has so often reported the Sychar meetings in the Holiness papers, and worked so faithfully for years as a board member, that he is surely enrolled as a part of the Sychar family.

In 1890 there were memorial services for that old warrior of the Cross, Sheridan Baker. He had left his frail, disease-racked body at the summons of His Master, to stand in His presence with joy forever more. It is noteworthy that as this founder of the "School of the Prophets" of the Association departed Joseph Smith appeared.

How often does it seem in the wisdom of man that some never-to-be-replaced warrior is called away, making an irreparable loss to the Holiness Movement; but the Lord has

JOSEPH H. SMITH

been slowly ripening another to take his place, and this one appears at just the right moment, to carry on. Men pass but God's work goes on. After Moses, Joshua; after Paul, Timothy.

In 1891 E. I. D. Pepper was an evangelist and A. P.

Howard was elected to the Board. The next year the Board began plans for a lodging hall or hotel. This was the first dormitory, which still stands.

In 1893 two notable names in Sychar history appeared. Beverly Carradine and C. F. English. Carradine's ministry for Holiness is a mighty chapter in the Movement all through the South. C. F. English and C. E. Cornell, who also were present in '93, were identified with young people's work at Sychar for a decade. Bishop William Taylor paid the camp another visit.

In the nineties it is heartening to note that the example of Rev. Reager was followed by the Gay Street Methodist Church pastors, and a close co-operation between church and camp was established to the enlargement of the spiritual life of the church. The names of Reager, Smith, Johnson and Barnett were well known on Sychar grounds as they led their people to camp and to the altar. The Methodist Protestant pastors of Mt. Vernon were usually also found to be in hearty sympathy with the camp meeting.

In fact, it may be plainly stated that all churches in a twenty-mile circle about Sychar could and can have the spiritual thermometer read as they reacted toward this mighty center of Holiness. Too often people take their pattern from the preacher.

When a preacher sidles into Sychar in an apologetic and deprecating fashion for one Sunday service; comes to the platform reluctantly, if at all; and slips out quietly before the altar service is well under way, one can usually safely state that his church is more interested in card parties and dancing than in revival services; that holiness is scorned as fanaticism, and the regular attendance at socials is ten times the prayer meeting figure. Out of such a church young people take a steady course toward the world, the flesh and the devil. In such a church the big men are most influential on two grounds only: money or social position. If anyone rises humbly to testify that the blood of Jesus Christ cleanses from all sin, the pastor's comment is usually sarcastic and repressive and leads people to believe that such a one is a fanatic, a trouble maker and a disturbing element, to be tolerated and kept as quiet as possible. Young people are taught to scorn such a back number. Those who stay true and maintain their testimony are treated with repression, rebuke and contumely.

It is sadly true that such a preacher and such a church too often have had contact with Sychar. It is a fearful thing to sin against light. People are either much blessed or greatly set back as they gladly receive or reject the truth of full salvation. More than one important national figure in our churches has been on Sychar grounds and, by reason of personal ambition, refused the convicting heart impressions of the Holy Ghost. Such men are today very much in the public eye; prominently mentioned for bishopric and other great appointments; their sermons quoted at length in newspapers and magazines; their voices heard often over the radio; great churchmen, national leaders in religion—and damned souls while still in the body. What a fearful reckoning these must face in the day of Judgment.

What a contrast are the preachers, who fall in love with Sychar on first contact. They advertise the meeting and pray for its success from early summer. From the earliest meetings they are present with a large group of their church members. Some they have brought already fully prepared as seekers. The altar call does not frighten away such a preacher. He turns to a hungry hearted parishioner and says, "Come to the altar with me, my brother." Down in the straw he prays and shouts and leads, as one after another of his own people find the land of Canaan. He testifies in the people's meeting; leads sunrise prayer meetings; and is seen arm in arm with the evangelist arranging a date for a winter campaign of clear Holiness preaching in his own pulpit.

Some of his people object and criticize; but he earnestly assures them that this is the way; that the straw of Sychar's altar may mean humbling of pride; but it sets one's feet on

the Way in the service of Him Who was born in the humbler
manger. The prayer meeting at his church grows. Testimony to full salvation gets a hearty "Amen, God bless you,
brother. Praise His name." The mid-winter revival stirs
church and town; his congregation grows and the Kingdom
of our Lord, Jesus Christ is advanced.

Thank God for such men of prayer as Reager, J. Frank
Smith and Barnett, who were not ashamed of the Gospel
of Christ.

In the nineties many great spiritual leaders made appearance in Sychar's old tabernacle. Bishop Thoburn, G. A.
McLaughlin, Joseph Gledhill, C. A. VanAnda, J. C. Fowler,
and W. C. Scuddy are but a few of the roll. Amanda Smith
was frequently present with her unusual ministry and fervent spirit.

America would never have had a race problem if the
spirit of Sychar had been the spirit of the nation. How
naturally, how courteously was a black woman given a place
according to her spiritual stature; without embarrassment
or condescension; in the real spirit of "in honor preferring
one another."

J. C. Fowler, president for years of the National Association for the Promotion of Holiness, often led at Sychar.
It proves the flight of time as it is remembered how he
looked on such young fellows as Joseph Smith and Henry
Morrison as promising youths, but scarcely fully proven
and experienced leaders yet. His was a commanding personality.

It was at the annual meeting of 1898 the first mention of
H. C. Morrison appears. He was invited for the 1899 camp.
The great team of Joseph Smith and Henry Morrison began
its Sychar appearances, as some of the older leaders such
as Fowler dropped out.

These were the days of the North Indiana Quartet, a
foursome notable for personal work as well as song. These
men sang from the heart and God greatly honored their
ministry in music.

As the new century emerges, in the record another highly honored name among the Holiness people of America became an annual feature of the Sychar program. A quiet,
demure figure in white bowed Deaconess bonnet could be
seen on the platform as a deep, thrilling, wonderful, voice,
accompanied by guitar, began "Ishi, Ishi."

That year the young people had a leader who largely increased the attendance. They flocked to Miss Iva Durham
as bees about honey. She never offered hasty time-serving
counsel. Each seeker was considered earnestly, prayed with
and counselled according to the oracles of God. One had a
sense of confidence in the analysis of one's own personal
problem. There was no compromise. If the truth were
hard, it must be spoken unwaveringly, but one could sense
real Christian love for one's soul's welfare.

Perhaps that is the reason why Miss Durham, now Dr.
Iva D. Vennard, president of Chicago Evangelistic Institute,
one of earth's great centers for holiness training, can travel
around the world and everywhere find men and women, who
were boys and girls brought to Christ under her ministry;
glad to call themselves still her boys and her girls. In Cey-
lon or Kobe; in the San Blas Islands or Chile it is "Mother
Vennard." Truly a mother in Israel, who has brought many
out of the wilderness into Canaan land.

In 1904 an unusual personality appeared on Sychar platform. The people of the camp have never been given to
worship highly placed people. Bishops have appeared in
numbers, but the title meant little. The test was: "Is he a
man of God? Is he filled with the Holy Spirit?" Education,
place, fame meant little if the answers were negative. This
year a product of a 'po white" family from the most backward and poverty stricken part of the South preached. His
grammar was atrocious; his figures of speech were chosen
from experiences that reeked of the soil. There was no
background of fine family or gentle upbringing. "Bud" Robinson boldly proclaimed his humble origin and confessed
that God raised him from the depths; forgave him his sins;

and, by the precious blood of Jesus, cleansed his heart from all sin and filled him with the Holy Ghost.

He was a powerful evangelist in those days of the fulness of his ministry, before denominational work absorbed his powers. He was never profound. In his peculiar lisp he would tell of the love of our Saviour, that could heal all our sins and lift us into holy living. Everyone sensed that he had been with Jesus and learned of Him. He knew the

C. L. LEWIS

Bible almost by heart and had the imagination of a poet. Many a man whom none other could reach would melt into repentance under Bud Robinson's preaching.

In 1904 another much loved member of the Sychar family appears in the records. Rev. C. L. Lewis led a sunrise prayer meeting. In the fall he was made auditor. His career, to end in years of the presidency, began.

CHAPTER VI.

THIS NEW CENTURY

The official records are very brief or altogether missing for much of the first decade of the new century. But memory brings back some names: Bishop Mallalieu, C. W. Ruth, and Will Huff. Each was present one season or more. Almost every year Joseph Smith was there. Fowler and Morrison repeated their ministry often. C. L. Peck, of Cleveland, and A. B. Riker became members of the Board. The Executive Committee consisted of Reager, Lewis and Riker. Mrs. Crouse had charge of the children. F. I. Johnson, district superintendent of the Methodist Church, moved to Mt. Vernon and, always in love with the true gospel, actively identified himself with the work. J. L. Brasher gave his impressive ministry. The great team of Joseph Smith and Henry Morrison became fully established.

The next decade showed new leadership appearing. Caton moved to Washington State and Oliver left Ohio. The Constitution carried a provision that automatically eliminated those not resident in the state. It was an attempt to keep an active Board, but sometimes lost to the Board an invaluable man.

The terrific disturbances of the four World War years saw only an expanding camp. People appalled by this dread visitation turned to God. As death swept Europe and then reached out his hand for America's choicest youth, who could fail to consider eternity?

A brisk, business-like, red-headed preacher named Miller brought a new type of message. C. W. Butler, now president of the National, made his appearance. His method was diametrically opposed to eloquence (and what a relief). But he was deeply read in God's word and his theology was as sound and deep as anyone ever heard. He took long for a sermon; but would stay at the altar until the last seeker

43

was through though it took until morning. And he got re-
sults, always.

What a diversity of methods is there among evangelists.
At one camp meeting an evangelist almost took a full second
hour for a very eloquent message. His call to the altar met
response. Within twenty-five minutes he was demanding
that all get through and leave. Twenty-five minutes for sermon and two hours for seeking would have been more

C. W. BUTLER

seemly. C. W. Butler never lost patience with a seeker.
The human soul is intricate in its workings; and, when lost,
often takes a devious path back to repentance and God.
The Holy Spirit is never in a hurry. Man may look with im-
patience and contempt on some poor youngster—or perhaps
an older person—because of frequent returns to the altar;
but "The Lord is merciful and gracious, slow to anger and
plenteous in mercy," and receives penitent seekers long
after people give their cases up as hopeless.

An evangelist in a hurry is a very unpleasant phenomenon. I have heard one spend his entire sermon time in telling personal anecdotes, all of which redounded much to his own aggrandizement. Somone said so and so. Back came the snappy, pertinent, utterly devastating reply. Incidentally such tales are difficult of credence. The experience of most people is that those brilliant answers come to mind several hours too late. After forty minutes of such relation, a brief exhortation preceded the altar invitation. Such shal-

PAUL REES

low fellows often bring back the report that the meeting was dead. Thank God, Sychar is seldom served by this type. Faithful men like Butler, Paul Rees, John Owen will expend their own strength like water poured out until the last sincere penitent gets through.

Camp Sychar has perennially the problem of the people who have to come to the altar every year for a period. The reason is not far to seek. For example, John Smith, a boy in his teens, finds the glorious experience of sanctification under the wise guidance of Sychar preaching and personal work. He returns home on fire to tell others of this inner secret of Christian victory. The first morning in his own home he faces a most difficult test. On his knees in his room he has promised God that he will witness before his parents. This is the hardest effort of a young Christian in a home where holiness is not experienced. Those parents remember when he stole apples and was caught at it. They can recall how often he shirked his household duties. It seems that surely every mean and sinful thing he was ever guilty of is immediately before them. He gulps and stammers in the most awkward phraseology, which later brings hot blushes to his face. "Why-er-ah, say folks—well—ah last night I went to the altar and got sanctified."

How utterly diverse from the rhapsody of thanksgiving and praise to God eloquently poured forth in the phraseology of his favorite evangelist that he had planned.

A chilly, surprised silence follows. The other children stare. Then father says, "Well, I hope you live it. Tom! Susy! stop that," and not another word on the subject. He goes out chilled to the bone.

At Epworth League he testifies to the blessed experience. But the whole church is cold and dead. Since the new preacher came holiness is distinctly an unpopular subject. The only ones applauded are those who say, "There is no such thing. Its just your imagination. The best people in our church don't have it or believe in it, and look how good they are."

So when this youth offers his halting testimony the preacher looks down his nose and several young people giggle. The leader says, "After all, I guess, what we need, all of us, more than anything else is to do our duty to our church and not spend too much time in unhealthy introspection." Nods of agreement.

John goes out a little separate from his companions in a chill of disapproval that could be cut with a knife. Not one word of encouragement or help. He is treated as one having some contagious disease.

Is it any wonder that he gets back to Sychar thoroughly lost out? He is hungry for his former blessed experience. No one who has enjoyed the fullness of the Holy Spirit can ever be satisfied in any other state. After a few days struggle back to the altar goes John. Then to the minds of many, and to the lips of some comes this, "There's John Smith again. I guess he's but a shallow sort. He does not seem to be able to get anywhere. This is an annual performance."

All honor to the perennial altar visitants who keep on coming until they are established. People may weary of them, but He who said, "Forgive until seventy times seven," is still on the mercy seat and doubtless He is weary of something entirely different.

Those who camped on Sychar's grounds will remember the Butler, Miller, Petticord preaching with Will Yates as song leader and Freese and Watkins, or the Mackey Sisters for special music. From the young people's meeting echoes of wonderful victory under the leadership of Edna Banning and May Gorsuch were heard. The last war year was the occasion of an unusual service. L. J. Miller led a patriotic service in which an American flag was dedicated.

The emotional stir of war days had this good effect. The Sychar attendance increased. In the face of such an holocaust of death people did give serious thoughts to eternity. The fearful death toll of influenza of 1919 and the serious thinking heretofore introduced, caused an increase of numbers, as reported by William Chase, of 55% over the previous year. Bishop Berry was present four days that year. Dr. Oliver, the former president of the camp, revisited Sychar.

On Sunday there were paid admissions of 3850. 674 autos visited the grounds. Very properly the Board launched its drive for an increase of plant to take care of the larger crowds. In the Sunday morning service L. J. Miller presented the plan and $11,000 was forthwith subscribed. The

money came with a rush. There was no painful pressing
of the issue. It was a body of cheerful givers; all of whom
seemed joyful for the chance to subscribe.

It is a noteworthy thing to be observed among really
sanctified people how their religion so completely absorbs
them that it reaches to and includes the pocketbook. This
is one of the three crucial tests of reality in experience.
How heart warming it is to encounter such an one. What
a contrast to ordinary church money raising. One calls on
Sister Smith, "The camp meeting (school, mission, revival
service) is in need of funds if it is to go on. Can you help
us?"

"I'm so glad you came to me. Let me see what is in
my tithe fund. Yes, and I believe I can add a thank offering
to the Lord at this time as well. He has so blessed my soul.
He has wonderfully cared for me materially. I am glad you
came. I appreciate the chance to contribute. Never fail
to see me when you need money. Let us have a word of
prayer before you go. Praise God. He is so good to us."

Exaggeration? Not a bit of it. This is almost verbatim
from personal experiences often repeated. Such a giver becomes a friend because of the request. This is in refreshing
contrast to those who count it an injury to be inquired of
for money.

Such givers were present in abundance that Sunday.
The new tabernacle was assured. The old structure was removed to the young people's location where it was long used.
The new tabernacle with sturdy concrete pillars supporting
a remarkable span of roof, without any inside posts, was
ready for dedication by 1921. Sunday, August 15th, Bishop
Berry conducted a solemn dedication service. As from the
beginning, "Holiness unto the Lord" became the keynote
for all services in this building. The altar remained plen-
tifully surrounded with straw, where earnest seekers after
God knelt, kneel, and please God, will continue to kneel until
our Saviour appears to call His people home.

In the first two years of the new decade there were several notes of the faithful regularly attending old saints who blessed Sychar with their testimonies, prayers and presence. Grandma English, 92; Grandmother Cary, 90; Aunt Hannah Lyon, 82; and Sister J. W. Hill, 82, are among those mentioned. Brother and Sister Malone, founders of Cleveland Bible Institute, grown feeble and worn in Christ's service, came. His voice was hard to hear at a short distance. But, oh! how the faith and loving devotion of his lips thrilled all of us who heard.

The increase of numbers continued to justify the building program. In the Jubilee year it was reported that 221 tents were engaged for the following year. In 1925 the report showed "embarrassing crowds." The Sunday crowds were larger outside the tabernacle than within. At times two ring meetings were conducted simultaneously with the regular preaching. This was the year when, due to two unexpected illnesses, E. W. Petticord had to carry the entire burden of preaching for three days, until John Owen could reach the camp. But he measured up to the crisis; and Will Yates sang, and led the audience in "All I need"; and the Holy Spirit was present in sanctifying power.

The evangelists of Sychar have mostly been men of God, preaching the Word under the inspiration of the Holy Ghost. But it is not altogether to them that victory is to be attributed on man's side of the work. Sychar has often witnessed a great altar service after a very feeble sermon. Audiences have sat, leaning forward with eagerness, just waiting for the sermon to end, to hasten to the altar from every part of the room, and there find the Canaan land experience of sanctification.

Why does this happen? The answer is to be found in hundreds of humble homes over the land. If you listen you will hear as early as June each year intercession with God for a time of mighty victory at Sychar. Men leading at their own family altars in uneloquent petitions, but with hearts on fire for souls, will mention each unsaved or unsanctified person in the family circle by name and ask God that this be the year that one finds peace. Moreover such men have ben giving daily witness by their lives to the truth of the experience of holiness. Their wilderness dwelling neighbors observe closely, and deep within their consciousness determine that they will seek and find this blessing at Sychar's altar.

Perhaps such a seeker hears very little of the sermon from the evangelist, but John Smith's eloquent life has convicted him to the depths. Such seekers make the altar service. John Smith is that tongue-tied fellow that kneels near; whose heard words are limited to a few broken phrases, as he travails with his friend. Smith is anything but prominent on the grounds, but what a mighty man of God is he for his community.

The shallow type of evangelist will report, "At Sychar I preached a powerful sermon and won seven converts and ten for sanctification." But in that great day of rewards the record will read, "To John Smith, at Sychar's altars, so many brought to God." He is one of those who "overcame him (the Great Dragon) by the blood of the Lamb and by the word of their testimony."

In 1927 there was a memorial service for many saints who had gone to receive their crowns. This has become an annual feature and, though a solemn, reverential hush falls on the camp at the time, many are blessed and rejoice as they note brethren with whom they have toiled are passed within the gates into that city. What a roll from Sychar. Col. Ball, Sheridan Baker, George Oliver, Fowler, J. W. Hill, Will Yates, W. R. Chase, Edna Banning, Amanda Smith, Martin, Skeen, Frank Smith, Reager, Dennis. Evangeline Ream will shine forth as the stars in the beauty of holiness. Amanda Smith, robed in white, with shining countenance will relate in detail the wonderful works of God she has experienced since going home. Will Yates will have some new verses about the golden bells of Heaven, for he is hearing them now. Sister Webb will shout and leap for joy; and many an one who was tongue-tied and bashful here, will eloquently pour forth the praises of our God and his Christ there, where the unending years of eternity pass in an atmosphere more filled with holiness than a sunny day is with light.

I want to be there, don't you? By the grace of God I mean to be there some day. For He who was able to carry them through to victory also has sufficient grace for each of us still on probation to the journey's end.

What a day of rejoicing that will be. W. R. Chase says, "Nearly every corner of the earth has those, who in the straw scattered around Sychar's altars have felt they heard God's call for some foreign field; and, in after years, have been back here to report their work among folks of foreign speech." One day they will make their report in full company; and to support their statements will be present those who heard their message of full salvation. Sychar's host in Heaven will be no mean company.

CHAPTER VII.

GREAT PREACHERS AT SYCHAR

While practically every evangelist of note in the Holiness Movement of America has at one time or another preached at Sychar, certain ones have so identified themselves with this camp as to be a large part of our story.

Foremost on this list is Sheridan Baker. Deeply afflicted in body, his soul was on fire for holiness, and his Sychar association extends from the first session of 1870 to his death. He preached at the first camp meeting and thereafter, whenever his health permitted attendance, he was prominent in activity. In an early meeting he failed to come because he stopped en route to visit a fellow preacher, found a revival started, and stayed on to help.

At the third annual meeting he was made vice president and shortly thereafter began work on the Executive Committee. In 1879 he was elected president of the Association and served three years. He served on the Board until 1905 or for 26 years. His zeal for soul winning was notable. He also stands out in people's memories for his holy common sense. At all times deeply spiritual and a profound champion of Holiness, he was able to combat any turning aside toward fanaticism. Sychar has in a remarkable way held firmly to the middle of the road; intent on its central purpose; the salvation of souls and the promotion of scriptural Holiness. To Sheridan Baker and his successors, under God, go the credit.

His family was likewise much attached to Sychar. His son, L. H. Baker, was active for years. Maggie Baker had the children's meetings from the beginning. Mrs. Oliver, his daughter, with her husband, G. F. Oliver, was very active for many years in children's and young people's services, song leading and personal work. Rev. Oliver was also president of the Board. It is sad that there are none of the third generation active at Camp Sychar.

George F. Oliver was a colorful personality. His driving

force added greatly to the success of the Camp. As president, with A. S. Caton for secretary, things ran smoothly. They had to for these men were energetic and able.

G. W. Dennis, George W. Ball and J. W. Hill were preachers of full salvation who carried weight in the Board and were active as soul winners and ever worked to advance spiritual zeal. All honor is due the Board of the O. S. C. M. A. Dennis, Ball and Hill are ensamples of the whole. Very often the members have been humble men so far as conference or ecclesiastical preferment was concerned. At times preaching full salvation was an assured path to demotion. So Board members of deeply spiritual richness went from town to village and to obscure circuits, while more pliable, less true men took the big city charges. This enriched the country districts beyond measure. Sychar preachers never complained but made any sacrifices cheerfully without whine. One old warrior of the Cross said, "I probably got quite as good churches as I deserved. Certainly I have no complaints to make. The Lord has been wonderfully good to me."

An experience of one of these Sychar saints is illuminating. Part of this story is not known to the man himself.

A certain sanctified preacher who for years had been active in all Sychar meetings, at the altar, in testimony and prayer, until he was thoroughly identified as "one of those Holiness fellows," accepted superannuation. He went to live in a new community and with his saintly wife joined the nearest church of his denomination. This church had at one time endorsed scriptural holiness and had had holiness evangelism under which most of the church leaders became seekers. But a preacher came in who began an active campaign against all this. A good mixer and clever politician, he slowly swung the church away until it became known as definitely opposed to all such doctrine.

So when Brother A. became a member a furor arose: "Watch out. Those people are fanatics and will start trouble sure. Best ignore them altogether," was the general cry. In the big women's class several said, "One thing is sure, we don't want that Mrs. A. in our class. She is one of those Sychar people." So instead of the usual calls and cordial invitation to become a member, she was cold-shouldered, as was he.

Both ignored all this. Perhaps they lived so close to the Saviour and were so filled with the Holy Spirit, that they had no time to consider slights and neglect. When one is truly crucified with Christ and dead to the world, certain things simply fail to register. They both quietly took their places in Sunday school and prayer meeting. Their prayers arose fervently, but they never sought leadership or prominence and steadfastly refused controversy. At all times faithful and unswerving in testimony, they had that God-given wisdom to know when to keep quiet. After such life-long identification with the Holiness Movement, they knew none could possibly question their convictions.

The alarm died down and those prophets of evil were soon proven false. Brother and Sister A. were so kindly, so humble, so sweet natured that a strong reaction set in. As so often the devil was caught in his own trap. His lies became so fully disproven by obvious facts that the pendulum of popular opinion swung strongly the other way. Sister A. was asked to become the leader of the very class which had feared her coming. He was listened to respectfully wherever he spoke. Sychar became much less a vision of wild-fire in the minds of all. Thus without effort these two won their place and sympathy for true holiness among a hostile people.

This is true heart Holiness in action. It works. Praise God the fruits of the Spirit do mature and appear to all. Such people filled with the Holy Ghost at Holiness camp meeting altars are professing "a good profession before many witnesses" all over America. They are indeed keeping "that which is committed to thy trust, avoiding profane and vain babblings." They will one day shine forth as the sun in the Kingdom of our Christ.

CHAPTER VIII.

REMARKABLE MEETINGS AT SYCHAR

To attempt to record the remarkable and outstanding meetings at Sychar would require several full volumes larger than this. The Holy Spirit has poured out blessing and victory without measure in so many seasons, that Sycharites are able to read Acts 2 with sympathetic and experienced appreciation. Every regular tenter can relate a score of impressive memories; and each person may recall a new set. Let old time campers at this point begin to recollect scenes of victory. Everyone who does so will have a praise service right there. Here can only be recorded a sample or two.

Altogether too much emphasis has been placed upon the shouting and uproar of a camp meeting. Detractors delight in exaggerating in this direction. The very man who will abandon all self-control and make a fool of himself with the wildest hullaballoo, when a winning touch-down is made in the last minute of play, looks down his nose at demonstrations under religious exaltation. One should be solemn and decorous in services—and inattentive—and spiritually in deep slumber.

At Sychar demonstrations of emotional outburst are not encouraged for their own sakes. But when the Holy Spirit descends in mighty power and a Heaven inspired shout goes up, it is the sweetest music in the ears of a true Christian. Sometimes it is misunderstood by members of more formal churches. But it is wonderful to note the smiles of approval upon the faces of the most sedate, as they come to the realization that this is Heaven-inspired. Much of the objection to this is born of a stinging conscience; for a lost soul becomes very forlorn in the presence of holy joy.

How many are as dear old Sister Webb, who, when she began telling her experience, was so overcome by the glory

55

of salvation that she must shout and leap for joy in a manner consonant with her exaltation of soul. One must be totally lacking in spiritual discernment who would fail to note the genuine heartfelt quality of this praise of our Redeemer. Such people would be very uncomfortable in Heaven when many angels and the beasts and the elders raise their voices, "Saying with a loud voice, 'Worthy is the Lamb that was slain to receive power, and riches, and wisdom, and strength, and honor, and glory, and blessing' "; for the numbers in that shout are reported in a certain record to be, "ten thousand times ten thousand, and thousands of thousands."

John Owen once preached from the first chapter of Ephesians on the Inheritance of the Saints. He demonstrated "the exceeding greatness of His power to us-ward who believe." He showed how we had been chosen in Christ "before the foundation of the world, that we should be holy and without blame before him in love." He opened up somewhat the glories of "the dispensation of the fullness of times," and lifted up before our eyes the kingly Christ at the right hand of God, "far above all principality, and power, and might, and dominion, and every name that is named, not only in this world but also in that which is to come."

As he reached his glorious climax and rolled forth, "with Christ through the ages, and the ages, and the ages of eternal bliss—," a might diapason of exalted voices accompanied him, as these saints of God were raised in thought to sit in heavenly places. "Glory to God," was the cry, "Hallelujah to the Lamb." No prolonged altar call was needed that day. People pressed to the altar as though time were at an end and eternity just beginning.

Time would fail to tell of the service where Miller's song book flew out over the audience, in perfect harmony with the exaltation of the hour: of the last night one year, when a Cleveland girl, a leader in a group of rebellious but sadly convicted young people, surrendered and then took the pulpit to exhort her crowd; until a second altar service, larger than the first, developed: of the missionary meeting where scores of young people dedicated their lives to foreign service (they are scattered over the globe this day) ; of the innumerable altar scenes of marvellous victory. One more scene must suffice.

Bud Robinson took a promise for his text one afternoon near the turn of the century. "Oh! yes," he said, "the Bible is full of promises. For example, in Genesis . . . ," and he quoted several verses; "In Exodus it says . . ." and several more. Book by book he went through the Old Testament, quoting everything by memory. Then amid increasing shouts of glory came the words of the four Gospels, and of the Epistles, one by one. The audience rose in an engulfing hallelujah chorus as he progressed. He started on the seven, "To him that overcometh" passages in Revelation; and finally in the midst of indescribable jubilation he quoted from the nineteenth chapter to the end completely. His two brother evangelists, usually very self-contained men in public, were walking up and down the platform together shouting the praises of our God and His Christ. Throughout the tabernacle the audience was leaping and praising God.

That was the whole sermon. He cried, "All who want a share in these promises, Come. The Spirit and the bride say, 'Come.' And let him that is athirst, Come." From every part of the room men and women fairly ran to the altar. Gospel hardened sinners, astream with tears, pressed forward.

> "And Heaven came down our souls to greet,
> While glory crowned the Mercy-seat."

CHAPTER IX.

THE HISTORIC POLICY OF CAMP SYCHAR

The folder announcing the first camp of the Ohio State Camp Meeting Association states:

OBJECT

"The special object of this meeting is the promotion of the doctrine and experience of Christian holiness, and we call the people together, not for the purpose of disputation and heated argument, but for the listening to plain Gospel preaching of the subject, and for the praying with and for each other, that we may promote the work of sanctification in our own souls, and so promote the salvation of the world."

From the beginning to the present day the main objective, "Holiness unto the Lord," has been the unswerving policy of Camp Sychar. Salvation of sinners and sanctification of believers above every other purpose is a sufficient program for ten days meeting.

The O. S. C. M. A. has never been controlled by any denomination, but has adhered faithfully to an interdenominational position, working with all evangelistic churches, but never seeking to build up exclusive membership in any one denomination. God has honored this stand, for He wants holy men and women, filled with the Holy Ghost, in every church as His witnesses. Many good men have felt that all sanctified people must join one certain denomination to be safe, but God has never put His stamp of approval upon such ideas. He wants a few faithful witnesses in every Christian Church and in the coldest, most modernistic setting there are His chosen ones, soul winners, zealous, centers of spiritual life. Praise God, holiness is a success under any condition, if the will stays surrendered to God.

This policy has led to many misunderstandings. In an early pamphlet the Association stated plainly it was not working to form a new church or to build a single denomination, but was seeking to send back men and women to the churches from which they came, filled with the Holy Spirit and perfected in love.

A RECENT BOARD

Sometimes injudicious altar workers have tried to turn aside. Statements have been made to seekers, or to those newly sanctified that they could not keep the blessing unless they left their old church and joined the counsellor's denomination. The Board has stopped such counsel when possible, and always maintains that sanctification is sufficiently real an experience to keep one on fire for God in any situation; that a cold church is much more likely to be set on fire from the burning prayers and testimonies of hearts cleansed from all sin, than to extinguish that holy flame.

Who is more honored of God than an advance guard in His army, placed in an exposed outpost to carry the great truth of Holiness to hungry hearts, where little or no preaching is? It may be more comfortable to be in a church where holiness of heart is honored and taught; but scriptural holiness would spread slowly indeed if all in the experience immediately separated themselves from churches, that might have no other witnesses to the truth, to enjoy the warmth and approval of those like-minded with themselves.

The Sychar type has even been a faithful witness in the midst of a crooked and perverse generation. To illustrate, there was a quiet girl who went to the altar at her first hearing of the doctrine and was wholly sanctified at the age of nineteen. She has never re-crossed Jordan. In the early years she witnessed in a community dominated by formalism. Faithfulness, as usual, was rewarded by rich fruits of the Spirit. She attended Sychar every year and her soul was warmed by the wonderful messages there given.

Then she moved to another town and joined a very large church, which at one time was true to the Wesleyan doctrine of scriptural holiness. Holiness evangelists had held many meetings with outpourings of the Holy Ghost on the people. Prominent leaders in this church had sought and found the blessing and witnessed thereto. But the enemy crept in. A few leaders backslid miserably. The church became notable for fighting all holiness teaching.

Miss A. had no great wealth nor family influence behind her in this church. She never wrangled nor argued, but steadfastly, unwavering, she stood her ground and on every proper opportunity, humbly confessed that "the blood of Jesus Christ, His Son, this day cleanses my heart from all sin." She was always loyal to her church and pastor, never critical. If the preacher spoke against holiness, she prayed for him and worked a bit harder with those who came to her for counsel. She never for a moment considered "come-out-ism" in any form. It would have been much more comfortable in an "holiness church" but she stood true to her outpost of duty.

Her reward was in this wise. A group of young people of this church were earnestly discussing this very point of doctrine. All but one in the group proclaimed loudly that there was no such experience. "You get it all when you are converted. Our preacher says so." "Look at Mr. B. He gives more money than anyone else and is a good man, yet he denies there is such a thing." (Mr. B. witnessed to the experience once but backslid and at this time was a pronounced holiness fighter.) "Those people at camp meeting just get emotionally excited for a time but it is not real and never lasts." "Look at old man C. He says he is sanctified, yet he cheated my father in a horse trade." "There is no such thing as sanctification."

Thus the conversation ran, until the one proponent said, "What about Miss A.?" The chorus without dissent, naively answered, "Oh! well, SHE'S GOT IT."

Praise the Lord Jesus. Those who witness for Him have their reward. This is a typical story of the wholly sanctified saints of Sychar who stand true to their God. Miss A. became the spiritual god-mother of all the young people of that great church who felt any urge toward Christ. And all her generation shall rise up to call her blessed.

This example is typical. An ignorant, ungrammatical woman in a city church became a center for the spread of holiness. A shy diffident farmer very limited of speech on any occasion, always of a retiring disposition, witnessed alone for years by testimony of tongue and life to this grace. From his community came a stream of seekers to Sychar.

An humble preacher in an obscure village charge preached holiness faithfully in the face of an indifferent church and a hostile ecclesiasticism. He got up parties of his people to come to Sychar and his reward was to leave a holiness loving church behind him. Sychar serves all churches and her teaching avails in any situation. Glory to the Lamb, that was slain. "These are they which follow the Lamb whithersoever he goeth. These were redeemed from among men, being the first fruits unto God and to the Lamb. And in their mouth was found no guile; for they are without fault before the throne of God."

The O. S. C. M. A. has ever been on guard against the wiles of the enemy. Satan knows he could make no progress by a direct attack on the central truth of Holiness preaching. So the subtle temptation has arisen time and again to turn aside toward some good and proper cause, profitable in itself. "We must study the Bible. Let us set up a Bible conference." "The great cause of temperance must be supported." "A young people's conference." "Let us center on missions." Such phrases have their appeal to many. But Spirit-filled men have stayed on their knees before God and guided by Him have never been sidetracked.

Some years after Sychar grounds had been purchased, certain good people proposed that the grounds be used for other purposes before and after camp meeting. Here was a beautiful grove with fine equipment and pure water in plenty allowed to be idle 355 days every year. It was a waste, they argued. It could be turned over to Epworth League conventions, Sunday school and Bible Conferences, meetings of various sorts for good causes.

But one said, "Surely among all the broad acres of beautiful Ohio there are groves in plenty for these worthy causes. Let us keep this ten acres dedicated to Holiness preaching. God will be honored thereby." The Board sustained him and this policy holds. Many a soul in temptation to turn back has returned out of season to Sychar's ground and there dropped on his knees, as sacred associations thronged his memory, to renew his pledge of full surrender to God; and as he took a farewell drink at the fountain, he has gone forth with benediction to victory.

Some complain of the narrow minded policy that keeps out pleasant harmless recreations. Surely tennis courts, croquet grounds, etc., would be beneficial and give a break to the strain of constant meetings. But Sychar's policy is that anyone can profitably spend ten days of concentrated work for God and Holiness, to the exclusion of every other activity. This practice keeps Sychar steadfast, unswerving, fervent, and God has blessed the camp mightily with the presence of the Holy Spirit.

In the tabernacle in printed letters is the challenge, "Holiness Unto the Lord." In the hearts of the people, in the activities of the camp; in every gathering and every resting time pre-eminently stands forth the one great standard of life: "Holiness Unto the Lord."

There is no more pitiful, and to a discerning mind, more tragic place than the site of a once mighty Holiness camp grounds now turned into a summer resort or Chatauqua grounds. To the spiritually minded such a place has the unwholesome, deadly miasma of a charnel house. Not far from Sychar is such a former camp ground. Once it was resonant with the groans of earnest seekers and the shouts of those entering Canaan land. To this day there are those who formerly went there still attending every summer. Such people are the outstanding champions of every Laodicean move in their home churches, and spiritually the place sends out only gospel-hardened scoffers against righteousness.

Better that an earthquake should swallow up Sychar grounds, obliterating them forever; than that the first compromising step be taken. God give to the present and future boards the same spirit of wisdom and discernment. God said to Moses, "the place whereon thou standest is holy ground," because He had manifested Himself there. Then surely Sychar is a holy place.

CHAPTER X.

L'ENVOI

And what shall we more say? For the time would fail to tell of each year, its victories and its testimonies. New evangelists, new singers, new tenters appear. Every year one notes gaps among the group, as some go home. That young man, just being tried out as a member of Sychar's Board, behold news comes that he has retired after years of faithful service in the presidency; and Brother Williamson will assume C. L. Lewis' place. Some will say, "No one can fill his place," as ever it has been said. But praises be unto our God forever, as one drops out another man of faith steps forward.

In spite of a thousand discouragements of the enemy; in the face of scorn and contumely, of ecclesiastical and social opposition, Sychar carries on. Obstinate and Worldly Wiseman oppose. Mr. Envy, Mr. Superstition and Mr. Pickthank bear false witness without. Pliable, By-Ends and Talkative within besmirch the reputations of all by their unfaithful lives. But Evangelist, Interpreter and Greatheart raise their voices without cessation. And yearly Graceless, Faithful, Hopeful, Old Honest, Young Mercy, Christiana, Valiant-for-Truth and Despondency with his daughter Much-Afraid take up their pilgrimage at this camp.

The world points with scorn at Feeble-Mind and Ready-to-Halt as typical Sycharites. The fall of every Heedless; the death sleep of every Sloth and Presumption, is blazoned abroad. Little Faith's misadventure and Mr. Facing-both-ways' hypocrisy are advertised; while Stand-fast, Mr. Holyman and Mr. Contrite are overlooked. All this opposes; but still over the platform, in the sermons, the prayers, and the testimonies stands forth boldly the glorious keynote of Sychar:

"HOLINESS UNTO THE LORD."

www.ingramcontent.com/pod-product-compliance
Lightning Source LLC
Chambersburg PA
CBHW020519030426
42337CB00011B/458